Exmouth and Budleigh Salterton

IN OLD PHOTOGRAPHS

Anne Carter and friends, Budleigh Salterton, *c*. 1887. In so far as any group in a community can impose an image on an age, for Victorian England that group was the middle class. They were the great success story of the era. Anne Carter, the beautiful young girl on the left, was the daughter of Dr Henry John Carter, who lived at The Cottage, Budleigh Salterton (now Umbrella Cottage). Anne died in Budleigh on 27 September 1949 aged eighty-four. Next to Anne is Mr E.W. Cave, the girl sitting down is Mabel Ross and next to her on the right is Geraldine Ross, the youngest daughter of the surgeon Gen. James Tyrrell Carter Ross (1823–97).

Exmouth and Budleigh Salterton

IN OLD PHOTOGRAPHS

Collected by TED GOSLING

Alan Sutton Publishing Limited
Phoenix Mill · Far Thrupp
Stroud · Gloucestershire

First published 1994

Dedicated to my new grandson Jordan

British Library Cataloguing in Publication Data

Gosling, Ted
  Exmouth and Budleigh Salterton in
  Old Photographs
  I. Title
  942.35

ISBN 0-7509-0394-5

Typeset in 9/10 Sabon.
Typesetting and origination by
Alan Sutton Publishing Limited.
Printed in Great Britain by
Redwood Books, Trowbridge.

Contents

Foreword

It gives me great pleasure to write the foreword to this excellent publication. Ted Gosling has produced a most interesting book covering the towns of Exmouth and Budleigh Salterton. The photographs, many of which have never been published before, show many aspects of the local life and how the towns have changed over the years. As far as Exmouth is concerned, it will serve to complement the work of others in providing a history of the town, while with Budleigh Salterton it fills a gap in the recorded past of the comparatively more recent town. This book will be most useful to residents and visitors in appreciating the changes that have taken place in both towns during their gradual development and growth. It represents a considerable collection of photographs brought together by the author, and it is a valuable possession for those who are interested in the past. *Exmouth and Budleigh Salterton in Old Photographs* marks another achievement in the author's efforts to create a pictorial record of the towns and villages of East Devon. All of these books are to be recommended to those keen to peruse the past of this delightful part of Devon.

Roy F. Chapple
Former Devon County and East Devon Councillor

Parade and beach looking east, Exmouth, *c.* 1920.

The Gardens, Madeira Walk, Exmouth, *c.* 1930.

SECTION ONE

Exmouth

Strand Gardens, Exmouth, *c.* 1935. A feast of colour throughout the summer, the Strand Gardens were laid out in 1870, and within them stands the town's war memorial.

Exmouth Esplanade, *c.* 1903. At this time Exmouth's claim to be regarded as a seaside resort was firmly established. The wide, asphalted promenade for pedestrians had seats and shelters where the visitor could sit in comfort, protected from the wind, from whichever direction it blew.

The Plantation, Exmouth, 1906. This attractive walk was laid out below the Beacon.

Exmouth Pier and Pavilion, *c.* 1904. At this time the pier served as the landing-stage for pleasure steamers such as the *Duke of Devonshire* and the *Duchess of Devonshire*. The pavilion was used for many activities, including musical and theatrical entertainment.

Exmouth beach, *c.* 1895. The fact that the children building sandcastles have hats on, and most of the older people are wearing hats and coats, is of no seasonal significance. In those days it was the custom of dress in warm weather as well as cold to conform with the strict social formalities.

Exmouth Golf Club, *c.* 1906. The club opened in 1886, with links on the Maer near Exmouth beach. It had one course with nine holes and a ladies course with six. The club suffered from flooding. The Exmouth council, which owned the land, refused to renew the lease in the 1950s.

Exmouth beach and Esplanade, *c.* 1895. At the height of the summer season the beach at Exmouth would be crowded with holiday-makers, many of them day-trippers from Exeter. At this resort there were many delights to please young and old alike. The noise must have been astonishing because, apart from minstrels and Punch and Judy shows, brass bands, hurdy-gurdy men and barrel-organs were all vying for attention. The policeman on the left is standing beside a street trader selling ice-cream.

The Esplanade, Exmouth, *c.* 1903. For a portion of its length the Esplanade is skirted by Morton Crescent. This view includes the Diamond Jubilee memorial and the clock tower.

Exmouth Sands, looking towards the docks, *c.* 1896.

Novelty seaside postcard, *c.* 1925. As well as the well-tried views, publishers of postcards produced an enormous number of novelty cards. This coy look from a bathing belle on a 'wish you were here' card was very popular for holiday-makers to send home.

Exmouth seafront, *c.* 1905. The clock tower was built to celebrate Queen Victoria's Diamond Jubilee in 1897.

Sydney Burrow, cycle shop, Exeter Road, Exmouth, *c.* 1901. Burrow, who began business as a plumber and ironmonger, drove the first motor car in Exmouth. With the coming of the car he opened the town's first garage, becoming a pioneer in this new form of transport. Here he is (centre) standing outside his shop.

Rolle Street, Exmouth, *c.* 1910.

The Strand, Exmouth, *c.* 1923.

Charabanc outing about to depart from All Saints church, Exmouth, *c.* 1926. The passengers had little protection against the weather, but convenience and novelty were the main attraction.

Exmouth Promenade, looking east, *c.* 1925. At this time the beach huts were erected below the sea wall, which caused problems during high tides and storms. They were resited on the Esplanade after the Second World War. In 1952 the council obtained permission to change the road into a dual carriageway, and so this peaceful scene disappeared for ever.

The Parade, Exmouth, *c.* 1914.

Rolle Street, Exmouth, *c.* 1899. Wickings the drapers occupied the shop on the corner with The Strand, and farther up Rolle Street were traders such as John Ridgeway, corn and forage merchant, John William Godfrey, nurseryman and florist, the dairy of Elizabeth Froom, and Harry Jessop the photographer.

The Imperial Hotel, Exmouth, *c.* 1955. This hotel, surrounded by its own gardens leading onto the Esplanade, was built in 1869 and added to in 1883. In 1903 it was enlarged, modernized and fitted with electric lights. The hotel was first built to cater for the increasing number of visitors to Exmouth and today it is the town's premier hotel.

Park Road, Exmouth, *c.* 1923.

Chapel Hill, Exmouth, *c.* 1911. The landlord of the Pilot Inn was William James Axon. The restaurant to the left of the inn was demolished before the Second World War. The new building, originally a newspaper office, is now a restaurant again.

Exmouth post office, *c*. 1907. At this time the town's post office was in The Parade, on a site now occupied by the Oasis Shopping Centre. The postmaster was Ernest Clark Pye and business was transacted from 7.00 a.m. to 9.00 p.m. In those days delivery was the most important part of the service, and Exmouth town had four deliveries a day: 7.00 a.m., 10.15 a.m., 3.30 p.m. and 6.25 p.m., with one delivery on Sunday morning. Letters for the 6.30 a.m. post would be delivered to London the same day, a service unheard of today.

Exmouth railway station, *c.* 1960. The original station was demolished in 1926 and replaced by this red-brick building, designed by Sir William Tite. This in turn was demolished in 1970 and replaced by the smaller station of the present day.

Telephone: 373.   EXMOUTH

THE LITTLEHAM GARAGE

Depot for
P E T R O L - O I L S & c.
Between Budleigh Salterton & Exmouth

CARS for HIRE
ANY HOUR & DISTANCE

CYCLES REPAIRED & ACCESSORIES

Advertisement for The Littleham Garage, *c.* 1928.

The Strand, Exmouth, *c.* 1909. The Strand Gardens, on the right, were given to the town by the Hon. Mark Rolle in 1870. The Wilts and Dorset Bank, on the corner, is now occupied by Lloyds Bank.

The Barn, Foxholes, Exmouth, *c.* 1900. Designed by E.S. Prior, this building burned down on 4 October 1905.

Clapps Café and bakery, Rolle Street, Exmouth, *c.* 1927.

The council stables and pumping station, Exmouth, *c.* 1969. The building on the right is now the Exmouth Museum, which was opened by Lord Clinton.

Thorns Commercial Temperance Hotel, Station Parade, Exmouth, *c.* 1906. The Temperance Hall in this hotel was known as the Coffee Palace. The proprietor, James Thorn, held various entertainments there, including the popular 'Saturday Evening for the People' concerts. In the 1920s the hall became a cinema.

The beach, Exmouth, *c.* 1889. At this time Morton Crescent, in the background, was of comparatively modern construction. The Imperial Hotel was built in 1869. The Bath House stood on the site of the present Deer Leap.

Looking down Rolle Street, Exmouth, *c.* 1910. Construction of this street commenced in about 1864, with the first shop opening in 1868.

The blitzed site, The Cross, Exmouth, *c.* 1948. This site now houses the Magnolia shopping centre, Frisbys is occupied by Dunns, the gents outfitters, and Denise is now a fruit and vegetable shop.

Withycombe village, *c*. 1910. At this time Withycombe Raleigh was a parish and village under the control of the Exmouth UDC. Although most of the buildings have changed, the Holly Tree inn still remains today. The landlord at that time was Peter Stocker.

The Primitive Methodist church, Exmouth Parade, *c*. 1912. This church, rebuilt in 1890, had seating for three hundred people. At this time this branch of the evangelical movement, started by John Wesley, attracted a large congregation in the town. The church was demolished in 1966 to make way for a supermarket.

Aerial view of
Exmouth town
centre, *c.* 1952.
Note the bomb-site,
now part of the
Magnolia Centre.

Exeter Road, Exmouth, *c.* 1930. Although this was the main road out of Exmouth,
there were no traffic problems as exist today.

The Manor Grounds, Exmouth, *c.* 1900. These grounds were opened in 1896, providing an attractive amenity for the town.

St Luke's Home, Exmouth, *c.* 1911. This convalescent home stood at the end of Alexandra Terrace, on the corner of Morton Road.

James Pulsford, drapers, 15 The Parade, Exmouth, *c*. 1912. James Pulsford kept a linen and drapery shop on the corner of Exeter Road and The Parade. His distinctive premises were a landmark in the town, and clients enjoyed a service that would not be thought possible today. During his time the shop offered the traditional qualities of good manners and service.

Woodville Road, Exmouth, *c*. 1956. How much easier it was to park in those days.

Exmouth open-air swimming pool, *c.* 1935. This pool was opened in 1932, remaining open for fifty years until the indoor pool was opened at the new sports centre.

Exmouth beach, *c.* 1922. This is a typical scene of tea huts, deck-chairs, people building sandcastles, bathers, paddlers and all of the seaside activities found in Exmouth.

Chapel Street, Budleigh Salterton, *c.* 1957.

South Parade, Budleigh Salterton, *c.* 1905. At this time Ernest Curry lived at Lochiel Lodge and Mr C.S. Turner was the secretary of the Gentlemen's Club on the left. This club was well situated and offered extensive views of the sea and coast.

Looking down High Street, Budleigh Salterton *c*. 1910.

The Rolle Arms Hotel, Budleigh Salterton, *c*. 1897. At this time the Rolle Arms Hotel was a first-class family and residential establishment, with a spacious lounge and drawing-room. The hotel had every comfort, and on the lawn facing the sea were tennis-courts and a croquet lawn.

The beach, Budleigh Salterton, *c.* 1954. A low-slung canvas and wooden deck-chair was essential for anyone who wanted to relax on the beach in comfort, while the painted wooden beach huts were useful for changing.

The river, Budleigh Salterton, *c.* 1955. Near the mouth the River Otter glides between banks of mud and, when the tide is low, sea birds gather here. In the background the dark firs give the impression of a natural wall.

The Church of St Peter, 1958. This church was erected in 1893 at a cost of £10,000, defrayed by the late Hon. Mark G. Kerr Rolle. It is a building of limestone nobbling with Monk's Park and Doulting dressings in the early geometrical Decorated style, and was built to the design of Mr G.H. Fellowes Prynne, a London architect.

Looking down Coastguard Hill, Budleigh Salterton, *c.* 1952. The car is a Morris Minor saloon. A vehicle remembered affectionately by all who owned one, the sturdy 918cc Morris Minor, launched in 1948, was designed by Alec Issigonis. By the time it was discontinued at the close of the 1960s more than 1½ million had been sold.

Fore Street, Budleigh Salterton, *c.* 1939. Parkers Café, which stood on the corner of Rolle Road, was an establishment known for good service.

Station Road, Budleigh Salterton, *c.* 1910. Once a country road called Moor Lane, this road was widened and renamed when the station was built.

Budleigh Salterton from the west, *c.* 1937.

Fore Street Hill, Budleigh Salterton, *c.* 1956.

Ash Villa, Budleigh Salterton, *c.* 1930. Ash Villa was built by James Lackington in 1812, and he lived there until his death in 1815. The house was pulled down in 1955 to make way for the present-day car park. James was the largest secondhand bookseller of the eighteenth century. He was born in Somerset in 1746, the son of a poor shoemaker, and it was not until 1769, when he was twenty-three, that he taught himself to write. He moved to London and opened his first bookshop. He became famous and successful, and in 1794 moved to larger premises in Finsbury Square, calling the shop The Temple of the Muses. The building later became the head office of the London and Manchester Insurance Co., before it moved in 1976 to Clyst St Mary. James retired to Budleigh Salterton and died there in his seventieth year.

The drinking fountain, West Hill, Budleigh Salterton, *c.* 1902. The fountain, which stood by Fountain Hill, provided water for horses and cattle.

Advertisement for Marks' Café, Budleigh Salterton, 1928. John Marks, the baker, was noted for his confectionery. His establishment had a most elegant interior and was more worthy to be called a restaurant than a café.

Links Road, Budleigh Salterton, 1918. These houses were built in 1900 by Fred Cowd. The road leads to the East Devon Golf Club.

The Octagon House, Budleigh Salterton, *c.* 1959. This is famous as the house where Sir John Millais painted the picture that everybody knows, *The Boyhood of Raleigh*. The picture shows two boys on Budleigh beach, listening enthralled to an old seaman's yarn. One of the boys is Walter Raleigh and the other is Humphrey Gilbert.

High Street, Budleigh Salterton, *c.* 1946. The King William Hotel is on the left.

Red-brick Georgian houses, East Terrace, Budleigh Salterton, *c.* 1900.

Budleigh Salterton High Street, *c.* 1902. You can see by the lamp standard on the right that there was street lighting at this time. This was provided by the Budleigh Salterton Gas Company, whose secretary at that time was Arthur Harry Passmore, with offices in High Street.

Budleigh Salterton, *c*. 1860. The building on the far right of the row in the background was the coastguard station.

Chapel Street, Budleigh Salterton, *c*. 1900. The serenity of this scene is in strong contrast with the Budleigh of today. People could stand in the streets without danger of being knocked down, and the din of modern road traffic was not there to dull the senses.

The beach, Budleigh Salterton, *c.* 1955. Note the crab pots on the beach beside the two young ladies, who are sunbathing.

River Otter, Budleigh Salterton, *c.* 1954.

Looking up Coastguard Hill, Budleigh Salterton, *c.* 1955. The large house on the right is Ottermouth House, which was demolished and replaced with the present-day flats named Blueberry Downs. At the bottom of the hill were the old limekilns. Once a local industry, lime burning stopped in the 1870s. For many years it played an important part in the history of the town, the lime being used for cement in building, lime wash (a form of paint) and for spreading on the county's acid soil. The car park is named after the limekilns.

Looking down Coastguard Hill, Budleigh Salterton, *c.* 1951. The café and beach huts were operated by the Gooding family. The Rosemullion Hotel is in the background.

Cliff Walk, Budleigh Salterton, *c*. 1949. The thatched summer-house belonged to the Rolle Arms Hotel, which at this time was the premier hotel in the town. For many years the Rolle Arms Hotel was the venue for many social functions and meetings, and it was a much respected hotel in the best of traditions, playing an influential part in local life.

Fore Street, Budleigh Salterton, *c*. 1950.

Budleigh Salterton, looking west from the West End bathing station, *c.* 1936.

Budleigh Salterton and the bay from Rosemullion Hotel, *c.* 1938. One of the town's leading hotels, the Rosemullion was demolished in the 1980s. Today this is the site of luxury flats.

Victoria Place, Budleigh Salterton, *c.* 1899.

Budleigh Salterton, *c.* 1892. The Gentlemen's Club is on the left. Judging by the people looking at the brook there must have been a flood that day.

Perriam's grocer and provisions merchant, 23 Fore Street, Budleigh Salterton, *c.* 1910. Mary Perriam ran this shop. She and her staff, here wearing the traditional long white aprons, were truly old-fashioned grocers. Their civility and charm are qualities sadly lost in this age of vast supermarkets. No doubt as one passed one would have noticed the delicious aroma of coffee, mixed with the smell of the smoked bacon and spices.

Looking up Fore Street, Budleigh Salterton, *c.* 1895. The Coffee Tavern notice is on the left.

River Otter, Budleigh Salterton, *c.* 1951. The praises of Budleigh and those of the Otter were sung by the poet Coleridge, who knew and loved them both well, being a native of Ottery St Mary. In the centre of the background are the gasometers at the old gasworks, which stood on the corner of Stoneborough Lane. The streets of Budleigh were first lit with gas in 1867, an innovation marked by a procession through the town.

Fore Street, Budleigh Salterton, *c.* 1952. Ash Villa, the house on the right, was once the home of James Lackington the bookseller. It later became the Temple Methodist Manse, but was unfortunately demolished in 1955 to make way for the Temple Manse car park. The streets of Budleigh were more peaceful in those days and the roads far less dangerous.

The West End bathing station, Budleigh Salterton, *c.* 1948.

General view of Budleigh Salterton from the west, *c.* 1935.

Queen Street National School, Budleigh Salterton, *c.* 1902. The Education Act of 1902 assured an education for every child. At this time the majority of Budleigh children went to this school. The headmaster, Mr Griffin, is on the left. The local policeman is also present. The school closed in 1912 and moved to St Peters Church School in Moor Lane.

Destruction on the beach at Budleigh Salterton caused by gales, summer 1910. Severe gales swept the Devon coast. Much damage was also suffered in the seaside towns of Seaton and Sidmouth.

SECTION THREE
The Villages

East Budleigh, *c.* 1894. The church in the background stands high, and its lofty tower looks down on a village of thatch. Sir Walter Raleigh was born near here in a farmhouse called Hayes Barton, and his father was churchwarden at the church. The stream on the right runs through the village and has never been known to dry up.

Alfords Farm, Exton, *c.* 1912. This charming farmhouse, on the main road to Exeter, was at this time the residence of John Alford, who farmed in the area.

Exton village, *c.* 1920. The cottage on the far left burned down during the Second World War.

General view of Lympstone, *c.* 1910. The Church of the Nativity of the Blessed Virgin Mary is on the right.

Cottages at Pretty Corner, Long Meadow Road, Lympstone, *c.* 1911.

The waterfall, Lympstone, *c.* 1914.

Littleham village, Exmouth, *c.* 1904. The forge of Billy Hillman was next to the thatched cottage on the bridge. The thatched cottages against the churchyard wall in the background were Violet Cottages, which were demolished in the 1930s.

Ladram Bay, *c.* 1895. This picturesque spot to the east of Otterton, much visited by tourists, was once a Benedictine priory. In the reign of King John it was a cell to the Abbey of Mont St Michel in Normandy.

Woodbury, *c.* 1898. At this time the population of this large village near the estuary of the River Exe was 1517. The church of St Swithin, on the left, was an ancient building of stone in the Decorated and Perpendicular styles, with an embattled western tower, erected in 1408.

Withycombe Mill, *c*. 1904. The splash of water and the turning of the wheel were the delights of this mill, which produced stoneground flour the traditional way. The Long family worked the mill for many years, but in 1962 the building was demolished. The wheel was removed and preserved in the gardens at the end of the Madeira Plantation.

Hayes Barton, *c*. 1910. A mile from East Budleigh is this house, in which Sir Walter Raleigh was born in 1552. It is now a farmhouse, nestling in a charming wooded dell. Its thatched roof is broken by three gables, and mullioned windows and a pillared porch add charm to the Tudor architecture. Sir Walter Raleigh was born in a room at the top of the winding staircase at the west end of the house.

Lympstone railway station, *c*. 1909.

The Church of St Mary, Lympstone, *c*. 1901. This is a building of red sandstone in the Perpendicular style. The embattled western tower, dating from 1409, contains a clock and six bells. At this time the living was held by the Revd Charles Gordon Browne, DD, of Balliol College, Oxford. He was also the rural dean of Aylesbeare.

Otterton church and bridge, *c.* 1899. The Church of St Michael was rebuilt by Lady Rolle in 1871, at a cost of £12,000, under the direction of Mr Benjamin Ferrey, FSA.

Otterton village, *c.* 1908. The lovely old thatched cottages were demolished in 1938, to be replaced by the modern houses of today. On the right is the post office, which was extended in the 1920s.

Otterton village, *c.* 1896. Otterton is situated on the eastern bank of the River Otter. At this time Lord Clinton was lord of the manor and the principal landowner, and the population was 622.

Knowle village, Budleigh Salterton, *c.* 1899. This is a scene typical of rural England before the motor car.

The Cliffs, Sowden End, Lympstone, *c*. 1910.

Salmon nets drying at Lympstone, *c*. 1910.

The Tea Bungalow, Woodbury Common, *c.* 1938. This opened just after the First World War and continued trading until its closure in the 1980s. Many will remember the wonderful cream teas served by Mrs Dupain and her staff – lashings of cream, homemade scones, cakes, scotch pancakes and jam. Every visitor always found courtesy, attention and good value, and anyone who ever paid a visit to the Tea Bungalow will agree that it served the best cream teas in Devon.

Lympstone, *c.* 1890. Looking across Greenhill Avenue to Burgmans Hill.

Littleham village from the bridge, *c.* 1935. The church of St Margaret and St Andrew in the background was restored in 1884. Lady Nelson, the widow of the great admiral, is buried in the churchyard. She died in London on 6 May 1831, having resided for many years at 6 The Beacon, Exmouth. There are also monuments in the churchyard to the Peel family, who were relatives of the great statesman Sir Robert Peel.

Knowle village, Budleigh Salterton.

Ladram Bay from High Peak, *c.* 1955.

Ladram Bay, *c.* 1925. This bay, about a mile east of Otterton, was a favourite place for picnic parties.

Sandy Bay, Exmouth, *c*. 1947. Although popular with the first postwar holiday-makers, only a few buildings occupied the bay area compared with the large holiday complex of today.

Sandy Bay, Exmouth, *c*. 1960.

Kersbrook, a small hamlet between Budleigh and East Budleigh, summer 1895.

The Green, Lympstone, *c.* 1900.

SECTION FOUR

The People

Florence Rose Hickmott, 1932. Florence was born on 29 December 1915 and lived in Exeter Road, Exmouth. She was a candidate for Exmouth carnival queen when she was only fifteen, and, though she did not win the crown, she was a 'maid of honour'. Nicknamed 'Fluff', she left Exmouth to become a dental nurse. She died on 3 February 1984.

Budleigh Salterton Rugby Team, c. 1899–1900. Although the team has no cup to display, their faces show a confident pride in their past and future achievements.

Budleigh Salterton Town Band, outside the Church Institute, Station Road, Budleigh Salterton, c. 1930.

Committee members of Budleigh Salterton Swimming Club, *c.* 1912. Left to right: Mr Worth, Mr Ellis, Col. Rowlandson, Dr Semple, Revd Rees Price (vicar of Salterton).

Porbeagle or bottlenose shark, *c.* 1910. This shark was caught by Walter Marker, who lived in West Hill, near Budleigh Salterton. Left to right: Walter Pearcey, Joe Ford, Charlie Pearcey, Frank Saunders, Fred Marker, George Potter, Jack Davie, Fred Wilson, Norman Pengilley, -?- (bank clerk), John Marker, George Pearcey, Violet Leaman (later Mrs Cleary).

Officers of the Home Guard, Exmouth and Budleigh district, *c.* 1944. Here, in the garden of The Lawn at the extreme end of West Terrace, Exmouth, Palmer House now stands. Front row, left to right: Lt. H.S. Sutherland, Lt. A. Beach, Lt. C.R. Rickeard, Capt. A.C.G. Roberts, MC, Maj. J.W. Palmer, Lt. R.T. Anderson, Lt. S.C. Caffyn, Lt. A.R. Smith, Capt. T.C.C. Evans, DSO. Back row: Lt. J.M. Pavey, Lt. W.A. Ingham, 2nd Lt W.A. Britton, 2nd Lt. A.F. Pratt, 2nd Lt K.H. Coxe, MC, Lt. J.F.R. Richards.

No. 2 (Budleigh Salterton) Platoon, A Company, 2nd (Clyst) Battalion, Devonshire Regiment Home Guard, at Highbury on the seafront, Exmouth, *c.* 1943. Front row, left to right: L/Cpl. L.W. Weaver, L/Cpl. G.L. Brown, Pte. I. Collier, Pte. R. Stainer, L/Cpl. W.G. Prew, L/Cpl. P.J. Hunt. Second row: Cpl. J.H. Parker, Cpl. P. Gooding, Cpl. C.E. Mears, Cpl. F.J. Spargo, ?L/Sgt. D.G. Mears, Sgt. E.W. Endicott, Pl? Sgt. G.H. Hayward, 2nd Lt. K.H. Coxe, MC, Lt. S.C. Caffyn, 2nd Lt. W.A. Britton, Sgt. W. Harris, Sgt. A.H.M. Jacoby, ?L/Sgt. W. Pratt, Cpl. G. Willis, Cpl. B.G. Smith, Cpl. C.A. Smith, Pte. F.B. Smale. Third row: Pte. H.L. Harris, Pte. F.W. Preston, Pte. F.J. French, Pte. J.H. Vanstone, Pte. J.E.G. Erskine, Cpl. A.H. Boxall, Pte. G. Grant, Pte. R.L. Pearcey, L/Cpl. G. Widdicombe, Pte. A.E. Chard, Pte. H.H. Fowler, Pte. J.J.E. Statham, Pte. W.F. Gooding, L/Cpl. W.J. Eales, Pte. D.H. Pidgeon, L/Cpl. H.A. Sellek, L/Cpl. A.C. Baker. Fourth row: L/Cpl. W. Beer, Pte. G.J. Jackson, Pte. A.G. Tonkin, Pte. R.W. Smith, Pte. H. Carnell, Pte. C.J. Fayter, L/Cpl. W. Selley, L/Cpl. G.D. Clarke, Pte. J.R. Bowles, Pte. G.H. Mears, Pte. A.C. Ellis, L/Cpl. H.G. Brookes, Pte. R. Stone, L/Cpl. J.E. Morris, Pte. P. Bolton, Pte. J.W. Williams, Pte. W.J. Goodheart. Back row: Pte. P.A. Rendell, Pte. C.F. Sage, Pte. R.W. Sellek, L/Cpl. R. Pratt, Pte. E.F.Watts, Pte. E.E. Hayman, Pte. T.V. Foley, Pte. C. Acland, Pte. L.H. Burch, Pte. K.H. Sellek, Pte. S.J. Westlake, Pte. F. Alford, Pte. M.B. Keslake, Pte. F.W. Powlesland, Pte. F.C. Keslake.

Tommy Bickford. Tommy owned a chemist on The Strand, Exmouth. After his death in 1907 aged seventy, the shop was run by Mr John Bickford.

Respectable-looking Exmouth couple, c. 1903. Nothing is known about the identity of these people. It is clear from their bearing that they were pleased to pose for the camera, and we are left with an image caught from a time when the elderly lacked the security of the welfare state and lived in fear of the workhouse.

Philip F. Rowsell, JP, FCS, a manufacturing and wholesale chemist, and the head of Holman Ham Co. Philip lived at Nutbrook, Withycombe Raleigh, Exmouth, and was born in 1864. A distinguished man, he was a member of the Council of the Pharmaceutical Society, chairman of the Chemist Defence Association of Great Britain, a member of the Wesleyan Church, president of the Exmouth Liberal Association and vice-president of the Exmouth Free Church Council. A man ahead of his time, he was interested in antiquarian subjects.

Thomas Hallett, who was born at Lympstone in 1846 and farmed Marpool Farm, Withycombe Raleigh, near Exmouth, for over forty years. Thomas was a member of Exmouth UDC from its formation, a manager of the Withycombe National School for over thirty years, an overseer of the parish and a member of the Exmouth School Board. He was the Peoples Church Warden for over thirty-five years and in 1906 was presented with a solid silver tea tray and two embossed silver fruit dishes from over a hundred parishioners in appreciation of his long service. A much respected man, Hallett officated as a judge for butter and cream at the Devon County Show, and his opinion was much sought after in farming circles.

The Revd Hervert Mackworth Drake, MA, Otterton, 1906. Revd Drake, who was born on 28 April 1870, was a descendant of the ancient Devon family, the Drakes of Ash House, Musbury. He was educated at Marlborough College and Keble College, Oxford, and was ordained as a deacon in 1893, becoming a priest the following year. He was the acting chaplain with the Devonshire Regiment in South Africa during the Boer War, and was awarded the Queen's and King's South African medals. A brave and much-loved man, he rescued people from drowning in the River Torridge, for which he was presented with the Royal Humane Society's medal in 1897 and clasp in 1898. He became vicar of Otterton, near Budleigh Salterton, in 1904. He was also a member of the St Thomas Board of Guardians and served on the UDC. There are two famous members of the Drakes of Ash family: the Duke of Marlborough was a descendant on the maternal side; before him, in the early sixteenth century, Bernard Drake was a famous seaman, who associated with such prominent sailors as Raleigh, Hawkins and Gilbert. He was knighted in 1585 but died a miserable death from a disease caught from a Portugese ship he captured and took into Dartmouth.

The Rt. Hon. Sir John Henry Kennaway, BT, PC, DL, JP, MP for Honiton Division (East Devon). Sir John Kennaway was born on 6 June 1837. He was MP for Devonshire (East) between 1870 and 1875 and for Honiton Division from 1885. A man of good judgement and vast experience, he was one of the most respected men in East Devon.

Exmouth mothers attending the welfare clinic, *c.* 1921. Just a few years earlier very little was provided in the way of postnatal care. The passing of the Maternity and Child Welfare Act of 1928 gave power to the local authorities to assist expectant and nursing mothers, and children up to the age of five. Some clinics were held in specially designed buildings, but most were held in church halls or clubs, and the premises were hired for one or two days a week. These local mothers looked forward to their weekly visits as a social occasion. The children were weighed and careful records were kept of their general progress.

This group of Exmouth people, taken in the 1950s, includes Eric Delderfield, Tom Fogaty and Mr and Mrs Parsons with their two daughters.

Ursula Perry at the back of Underhill, with the village of Lympstone in the background, 1946.

Exmouth beach, summer 1934. The lady with the hat is Marjorie Perry, the wife of local architect George Perry. She is pictured here with, left to right, family friend Molly Kedge, daughter Ursula and son Robert, who is proudly holding a splendid model sailing boat.

Miss Carpenter's Preparatory School, Budleigh Salterton, *c*. 1910. This school was situated in Budleigh High Street. When the headmistress, Miss Lily Mary Carpenter (centre), married Mr F. Kerslake, this photograph was presented to her to commemorate that happy event. Front row, left to right: Paul Perriam, Sylvia Piller, Winifred Bickley, Albert Raymon, Annie Burch. Middle row: Nellie Flew, May Bickley, Miss Mabel Beer, Dolly Cooper, May Trickey. Back row: Evelyn Trickey, Dora Perriam, Ethel Connett, Amy Marker, Norah Trickey, Beatrice Walker.

Miss Caunter's dancing class, Exmouth, 1935. Dancing academies were very popular in the 1930s and led to special tuition for the talented at local specialist schools. We do not know if these children were talented, but they all look dedicated and have responded well to the photographer in this charming picture.

Lympstone Home Guard, No. 2 Platoon, B Company, 2nd Clyst Battalion, *c.* 1943. The plan of raising Local Defence Volunteers in 1940 met with an immediate response from all over the country. Their name was soon changed to the Home Guard, although they were known affectionately as 'Dads' Army'. By the end of that year the Home Guard numbered 1½ million men, and during the preparations for D-Day in 1944 they took over most of the security duties in the country. These men from Lympstone played an important part in the Second World War, and, after their final muster in 1945, much appreciation was felt by all for the voluntary work they had done during the difficult days of the war. Front row, left to right: W.C. Barnes, F.W. Stevens, J.C. Norton, R.G. Adams, Dr G.S. Nichol, 2nd Lt. S.W. Thorn, Lt. O.L. Young, Revd B. Steinmetz, Sgt. R.J. Haydon, Sgt. W.W. Bryant, Sgt. W.R. Croft, Sgt. L. Hyde. Second row: R.G. Maddocks, S.A. Sommers (behind), ? Bell, M. Pyle, D.J. Clake, H.G. Lowman, A.C. Allen, F.G. Dunscombe, E.J.W. Pidsley, E.J. Bowden, J.P. Long, A.N. Pyle, C.E. Baker, J.N. Sherwill. Third row: Cpl. F.D.J. Blight, W.H. Pearcey, W.H.G. Newberry, B.J. Bolt, W.H. Corner, S. Sparks, T. Carder, H. Pring, L.H. England. Fourth row: E.G. Locke, W.E. Litten, A. Field, W.G. Morrish, R.N. Wannell, W.G. Hallet, A.D. Langmead, T.B. Stemp, R. Vanstone. Back row: Cpl. W. Webb, W.S. Norton, P.G. Snow, Cpl. S.E. Drew.

Group of workmen employed by the Exmouth Council in the seafront widening scheme, looking towards the Imperial Hotel, Exmouth, *c.* 1953. Left to right: Bill Jones, Walt Gooding, Charley Richards, Albert Slocombe, Mr Down, Bill Stredling, Cyril Hammond, Frank Griffiths (foreman), -?-.

Exmouth beach, 19 April 1967. Holiday-makers and locals would have seen them on the stage of the local theatre, but the appearance on the beach of these delightful girls from the Exmouth Operatic Society marked the opening of the 1967 Exmouth beach season. Certainly that year Exmouth could look for a successful summer, unlike many Devon resorts, which were suffering from oil spillage from the wrecked tanker, *Torrey Canyon*. No doubt these girls would have spent much of their leisure time on the beach. Left to right: Christine Hayne, Beryl Watts, Christine Field, Jane Crump, Reita Phillips, Sharon Firth, Pam Barrett, Iris Moore, Sheila Leat.

Robert Perry and his sister Ursula, Exmouth seafront, 1936. Robert and Ursula were the children of Exmouth architect and surveyor George Phillip Perry. The beach huts were at that time erected each season below the sea wall on the Esplanade, which always caused problems during very high tides.

Marine Drive, Exmouth, looking towards Orcombe Point, *c*. 1933. The Marine Drive to Orcombe was completed in 1920, and pictured here below the sea wall are Mrs Marjorie Perry and her daughter Ursula.

Pupils at Queen Street School, Budleigh Salterton, 1905.

Maypole dancers, Queen Street School, Budleigh Salterton, 1907. White-frocked girls with ribbons in their hair, and their serious-looking partners, prepare to dance around the maypole. This was once a colourful custom of all rural schools and an essential part of every village fête.

Thorn and Sons carriers. Based at 12 Union Street, Exmouth, this company provided a daily service to Exeter. They also had two horse-drawn pantechnicons for removals and were noted for their careful attention.

Fancy dress party at Clarendon Cottage, Exmouth, *c.* 1910. Children love dressing up, and the delightful group pictured here might have played a part in a school pageant. Those were the days of active participation rather than the passive watching of the present era.

Pupils at Miss Bannister's School, Budleigh Salterton, *c.* 1933. Miss Bannister (right of centre, back row), remembered with great affection by all who knew her, taught in Budleigh for over sixty years. The school stood on the site now occupied by Green Mews Flats.

Exmouth cockle woman with her rake and basket, *c.* 1897. At one time the mussel and cockle beds within the shelter of the estuary were of great importance to the local economy.

Humphries Smithy, Withycombe village, *c.* 1910. At this time the blacksmith played an important part in village life. This smithy was, unusually, owned by a woman, Mrs Sarah Humphries.

East Budleigh family group, Woodbury Common, June 1884. The family and the occasion are unknown.

Harry Rodgers and George Pearcey making crab pots, Budleigh Salterton, *c.* 1897. The fisherman on the left is making the flat base of the pot. The splendid looking character on the right is bending the withies over the form.

George Phillip Perry in the *White Heather* sailing-boat off Exmouth, *c.* 1926. George, who died on 28 January 1979 aged eighty-three, was an architect and surveyor who lived at Redcliffe, Burgmans Hill, Lympstone. He was the chief assessor of the South West War Damage Commission. His hobbies included sailing and gardening. He was a man of great integrity who inspired trust and affection in all who met him.

Marjorie Perry, Exmouth, *c.* 1924. The wife of George Phillip Perry, Marjorie died on 18 March 1987 aged eighty-five.

Players in Exmouth, 1924 season. Pier theatres provided a full season of entertainment for the visitors. Pierrots, who performed comic sketches and sang songs, like 'Just because the violets are shining in the lane', were very popular.

British Legion Children's Christmas party, church hall, *c.* 1955. The adults present include Mrs Thorn, Mrs Grace Burch, Mr Rowe and Mrs Crutchley.

The opening of Dotton Waterworks, Exmouth, 1911. The opening ceremony, on Tuesday 6 August 1911, was performed by Lady Clinton. Those present include Lord and Lady Clinton, Sir Clive Morrison-Bell (the local MP), Mr H. Blackmore (Chairman of Exmouth UDC), Revd Buckingham (Chairman of St Thomas RDC), Mr A. Kneel, Mr H. Crews, Mr J. Carter, Mr R. Tucker, Mr J. Cooper and Dr H. Martin.

Exmouth choirboys, c. 1900. The occasion was the Choirs' Festival. Front row, left to right: W. Burrow, W. Steer, H. Guscott, P. Clarke, H. Grace, C. Davey. Second row: -?-, W. Dunn, G. Ponsford, E. Surridge, H. Gooding, -?-, W. Hayman, -?-, B. Edwards, -?-. Third row: S. Burrow, A. Wills, J. England, P. Paul, E. Guscott, R. Wilmot, P. Snow. Fourth row: P. Perriam, J. Gidley, F. England, D.Taylor, T. Spiller.

Presentation ceremony, St John Ambulance Brigade, Bastine Hall, Exmouth, *c.* 1958. Front, left to right: Mrs Rex, Evelyn Juston. Back: Sheila Steels, -?-.

Exmouth Church School musicians at the Trinity church hall, *c.* 1937. This hall in Church Road was later demolished.

During the visit of HMS *Exmouth* in May 1960, a seat was presented to the citizens of Exmouth by the ship's company. It was placed in the Pavilion Gardens. Here the ship's captain is presenting the seat to the Chairman of Exmouth Council and other councillors.

Unknown occasion, 1950s. Local journalist Bill Gorfin is on the left. This is something of a mystery picture. One of the frustrating features of collecting old photographs for a book like this is the large number you find with no date or description. Any information on the occasion would be welcome.

Budleigh fishermen with a catch of herring, *c.* 1913. Before the 1930s the Budleigh Salterton fishermen caught mackerel and herring in shoals. By 1929, however, the local fishing industry was already failing, partly as a result of the sudden disappearance of the herring.

Mussel-cleansing tank, Lympstone, *c.* 1930. The edible sea mussel had to be cleaned in these tanks, which were built at Sowdens End in the 1920s. Here local fishermen are cleaning the mussels, which at that time were part of a major local industry.

Pat Hickmott, Exmouth sands, July 1942. Pat was born in 1909 and lived in Exeter Road, Exmouth. The barbed wire was part of the Exmouth beach defences during the Second World War. After the war Pat went to work as a personal assistant to the McCorquodale family, who are related by marriage to Princess Diana. Pat died on 26 December 1966.

Group of charming Exmouth ladies, 1950s. No details of the occasion or subject are known, so any information would be appreciated.

Exmouth Volunteers on Woodbury Common manoeuvres, *c.* 1865. Exmouth played a prominent part in the Volunteer movement, which was formed nationally during the Napoleonic Wars. Locally, F Company was formed in 1851, but it appears to have played a more important part in the social life of the town than in defence.

The East Budleigh bell ringers, leaving the Kings Arms (now the Sir Walter Raleigh), East Budleigh, for a day's outing, *c.* 1930. The driver, wearing the long white coat, was Bill Britton, who worked for Harts of Budleigh.

Children from a private school in Exmouth performing in the school pantomime, 1903.

Mackerel catch, Budleigh Salterton, 29 December 1906. On this day over forty thousand fish were caught.

SECTION FIVE

Events

George Street coronation celebrations, 1937. The big event of this year was the coronation of King George VI on 12 May. The new royal family presented an image of contented domesticity and the whole country celebrated the event with street parties.

Exmouth floods, 28 September–6 October 1960. Following an unusually wet summer, the last week of September was one of almost continuous rain. During the night of Thursday 29 September the exceptional downpour flooded the Withycombe Brook. The rain continued the following morning and by midday storm water caused the Brook to overflow, resulting in severe flooding in the Exeter Road area. Muddy water up to four feet deep poured into houses, causing much damage to furniture and carpets. Exmouth Council workmen, policemen and firemen waded in water that was waist-deep at times, giving aid where it was needed. Emergency pumps from the Fire Brigade were used to clear as much water from the area as possible. During the following days help came from the Royal Marines at Lympstone, the Wessex Brigade from Exeter and the Durhams, who were stationed at Honiton. Much gratitude was felt by the people of Exmouth for this help in their hour of need. Unfortunately, no sooner had the mess been cleared up than the whole chain of events was repeated. During the evening of Thursday 6 October a thunderstorm, with two hours of heavy rain, caused flooding in the area again. This time it was more severe, with at least a thousand homes affected, and once again voluntary workers, firemen, police and troops rushed in to help. On the Saturday the Parliamentary Secretary to the Minister of Housing, Sir Keith Joseph, and Lord Roborough, the Lord Lieutenant of Devon, toured the area. They were appalled by what they saw, but were full of praise for the local people and for all those who were helping to clear up. Top: the Royal Marines provide hot drinks for the people of Salisbury Road; bottom: this photograph reflects the British ability to find humour in the face of adversity – the man on the left could be saying, 'I'm a pump engineer, not a plumber.'

The floods at Lympstone, 1960. This is the lower Strand, with the post office in the background and the chemist on the left. The entrance to The Globe is on the right.

Trip by boat in Exeter Road, Exmouth, during the floods of 1960.

The group of workmen who built the first council houses after the First World War.

Exmouth floral queen and maids of honour, *c.* 1956.

Crowning of Exmouth carnival queens, 1950s. The colourful spectacle of carnivals is as much a part of the East Devon calendar as the seasons of sowing, harvest and Christmas. Before the Second World War Exmouth carnivals were a great success, with thousands of people lining the route. Showmen – including Anderton and Rowlands, Hancocks and Brewer – brought their fairs, and other entertainers flocked to the town, making a day of rejoicing and general gaiety. After the war the carnival continued to bring colour to Exmouth.

Chairman of Exmouth Council and other notables with the Exmouth floral queen, *c.* 1956.

First aid competition, Bastine Hall, Elm Grove, Exmouth, *c.* 1960. Those present include Maureen Campbell, Margaret Evans, George Coates and Mr W. Perryman.

Coronation meal, Phear Park, Exmouth, 22 June 1911. Although the country was passing through a difficult time and there was every sign of growing tension with Germany, the day of the coronation of George V was celebrated everywhere with numerous events.

Budleigh Salterton tennis ground, August 1893. At this time lawn tennis was becoming popular. The Budleigh Croquet and Lawn Tennis Club had excellent grounds, comprising seven tennis-courts and three croquet lawns.

Occasion unknown, Exmouth, 1950s. Any information on this occasion would be welcome.

Pupils from Exeter Road junior school, Exmouth, 1950s. A school board, formed in 1875, was responsible for erecting the school.

Members of Budleigh society playing croquet at Abele Tree House, Budleigh Salterton, c. 1895. It was during the latter part of the nineteenth century that croquet enjoyed a great social prestigee. At this time Abele Tree House was the residence of Dr Semple.

Following the Exmouth carnival procession in 1955 is the 'Appeal Van', requesting spectators to throw in their spare coppers.

Budleigh Salterton Town Band, c. 1908. Before 1914 every town had its own band. The Budleigh band was always in demand for local events, including the carnival.

Empire Day celebrations, Budleigh Salterton, c. 1909. Before the First World War, Empire Day was a school holiday and an occasion of much rejoicing. It was held on Queen Victoria's birthday, 24 May, and originated in commemoration of the assistance given by the colonies in the Boer War of 1899–1902.

Street parties to celebrate the coronation of George V, Budleigh Salterton, 22 June 1911. The coronation was an occasion of national rejoicing, and a full programme for the event was arranged in Budleigh Salterton. The streets were lavishly decorated and the day commenced with a service in Rolle Square. This was followed by parties in the streets, where tables and benches were set up and people sat down for a meal. During the day other entertainments took place, including children's sports.

The homecoming of the Budleigh Salterton Boer War Volunteers, 15 June 1901. Two men from Budleigh Salterton – Pte. Freeman and Pte. Morrish – volunteered and served in the Boer War. When they returned they were met at the local station by a full muster of their comrades from the Exmouth Company of Volunteers. Here, on the steps of the Royal Hotel, they were presented with celebration watches. Those present include Revd W.F. Green, R.C. Price, Mr R.W. Friend, Dr Brushfield, Dr Walker, Capt. Cooper, Mr H.C. Perriman and the following members of the council: Mr J.C. Palmer (chairman), Mr Marker, Mr Marshall, Mr Parsons, Mr Pidsley, Mr Bennett.

Memorial service for Queen Victoria, Fore Street, Budleigh Salterton, 1901. Queen Victoria died on the evening of 22 January 1901, surrounded by her children and grandchildren. The whole country was in mourning, with a universal feeling of loss and emptiness.

Public meal, George V coronation celebrations, Phear Park, Exmouth, June 1911. The summer of 1911 was remembered for the coronation and as a year when the sun shone from a blue sky almost without interruption. The whole country celebrated the event with sports and parties.

Street party celebrating the coronation of George V, Budleigh Salterton, 22 June 1911.

The *George and Mary* lifeboat going to a call out, Exmouth, *c.* 1955.

Fire at Exmouth, *c.* 1951. The house belonged to a Dr Murray and stood on the corner of Carlton Hill, off Rolle Road. The site is now occupied by a block of flats.

The *George and Sarah Strachan* lifeboat going to a call out, Exmouth, *c.* 1960. Built in 1931 for the Dunbar station, this vessel was a 45 ft 6 in long, non-self-righting lifeboat of the Watson class. It was transferred to Exmouth in 1960 as a reserve lifeboat.

Fire tender at the fire in Dr Murray's House, Exmouth, *c.* 1951,

Sector 109 Fireguards, Exmouth, 1944. Fireguards played their part in civilian defence during the Second World War. During air raids they patrolled various areas on the lookout for incendiary bombs. Front row, left to right: G. Howe-Haysom, W. Hall, A. Dommett, J. Southwell, H. Hynard, W. Bond, G. Hall, B.H. Avery (sector capt.), P. Milford, R. Ridley, A. Carpenter, L. Bradford, A. Moist, ? Moist, H.A. Johnson. Second row: D. Dymond, E. Madge, E. Letten, E. Smith, I. Tozer, L. Stubbington, M. Fryer, A. Roach, L. Underwood, A. Thompson, V. Dobel. Third row: M. Tucker, D. Seagroatt, E. Richards, E. Pidgeon, D. Salmon, L. Bell, E. Williams, M. Oxford, K. Maers, D. Southwell, M. Ridley, F. Humphries. Back row, left to right: H. Bond, A. Backhouse, M. Bond.

Chapel Street after the German bombs were dropped, 18 January 1941. Exmouth suffered many air raids during the Second World War.

Men from Budleigh Salterton leaving by special train, August 1914. War fever swept Britain like an epidemic and people could hardly wait to get to grips with the Germans. Those present include Jack Davie, Tom Burch, Alfred Knowles, Len Curtis, Bill Bennett, Walt Marker and Bob Easton. They left the station with those they left behind cheering, shouting, singing and waving goodbye with their handkerchiefs. It would be four long years before the war ended, and those that returned would find a country changed beyond recognition.

Exmouth Boy Scouts on parade, *c. 1956.* In August 1907 twenty boys, led by two men, pitched their tents on Brownsea Island in Dorset. The boys were gathered from all walks of life, and for two weeks they learned to live in the open and to cultivate comradeship. From this small beginning the Boy Scout movement was born, and Baden Powell, their leader, was on his way to becoming a world figure.

Exmouth dairy maid (centre), *c. 1957.*

Laying the foundation stone for the rebuilding of St Bernards, Exmouth Town Hall, by the Chairman of Exmouth Town Council, L.M. Lees, JP, c. 1958.

Crowning of the Exmouth carnival queen, c. 1954. The ceremony was performed by Arthur English.

The Yeomanry, training outside Tucker's shop, *c.* 1855. The old Exmouth market is on the right. It was built by Lord Rolle in 1827 and demolished in 1869. In the background is the second Exmouth post office. The Devon Yeomanry would arrive in the town for training, led by the fifes and drums. Large numbers of people would gather to see them come, and their officers would be billeted in the various hotels. Training was done in the summer between the hay and corn harvests. It began at 5.00 a.m. with a bugle call to muster, followed by two hours of drill. Rations were then served, which consisted of meat and bread. This they stuck on their bayonets and carried through the streets.

No. 7 Company RGA outside the Drill Hall, Exmouth, *c.* 1901. This building is now the leisure centre, on the site of the old Sailor's Rest. Note the King Edward VII sign on the building. On the left are Attwaters Imperial Stables, now Samantha's night club.

Coast Guard crew at a firing exercise, Budleigh Salterton, *c.* 1909.

Exmouth residents outside the Temple of Theseus on the visit of the Devonshire Association to Exmouth, summer 1928. The association was formed on 22 April 1862, and from the beginning held its annual meeting in various towns of the county. Those present played a prominent part at the time in the life of the town. They include Percy J. Barrow, Fred A. Farleigh, J.J. Summers (chairman of the council), Ben Benoy (clerk), Mr & Mrs H.E. Wickings, Mr H.T. Easton, Mrs O.J. Reichel, Mrs H.J. Greenwood, Professor S.J. Vines, Miss A. Barber, Mr & Mrs F.S. Wilson, Mrs Fred A. Farleigh, Mr W.T. Godfrey, Mr S. Hutton (surveyor), Revd Edward Peters (Beacon Congregational), Revd & Mrs Gregory Bateman, Revd John Thomas, A.H. Toone, T. Tozer, James Barber, W.H. Wright, A.J. Bulled, A.E. Humphries, Wallace Bardens, W.J. Delderfield, H.J. Appleby, Mr Fred C. Hunter, Revd T. Tizzard (Glenorchy), H.S. Carter, J. Drake, C.J. Berry, Mrs J. Jefferies, Mr & Mrs P.J. Dixon, Mr F.E. Drawer, Mr & Mrs R.N. Harding, Mrs Begbie, Mr & Mrs D'Arcy, W.A. Hughes, Mr H. St A. Sims, Mr E.P. Luke, Revd Preb E.V. Cox, Mr H. Mann, Mr W. Hickley, Mr Harry Ford, Capt. C.P. Shrubb, Capt. Richard Barrow, Mr R. Sowton Barrow, Mr P. Raymond Gibbs, Mr W.R. Park, Revd T.S. Lea, DD, Mr & Mrs G. Anderson, Capt. Owen Wethered, Mr W. Gordin.

Bill Britton, *c*. 1960. Bill Britton, who died aged 87 in 1985, was known and loved by generations of local people who travelled by coach. Commencing his driving career working for Sid Burrows of Exeter Road, Exmouth, he left in the 1920s to work for Harris's Garage in The Parade, taking people on the earliest charabanc outings from Exmouth. When Mr P. Hart started his bus service in Budleigh Salterton in 1927, Britton joined him and soon become a part of the Hart legend – all Hart's drivers and buses were held in great affection by the general public. He ended his working life working for Greenslade Tours in their Budleigh depot, and is pictured here as so many will remember him, with a friendly smile and wearing a Greenslade drivers' coat. The monkey was a photographer's prop, used in Newquay by a local photographer.

British Legion Dinner, Exmouth *c*. 1958. Taken in Exmouth's Pavilion, the group includes Mrs Dunn, Mrs Bedwell, Mrs Tozer, Mrs King and Miss D. Mann.

Man and barrel-organ outside the Feathers Hotel, High Street, Budleigh Salterton Carnival, *c.* 1910.

Budleigh Carnival, *c.* 1909. Carnival was a time for rejoicing and general gaiety, but judging by the expressions of these mounted entries, pictured outside the Rolle Hotel, they had not yet got into the spirit of the day.

Budleigh Salterton Carnival, *c.* 1933. Parading in the carnival with the old fire engine from Bicton are Charlie Jewell, Bill Searle, Jack Cooper and Albert Hitt.

Presentation of a certificate to railway workers, Budleigh Salterton railway, *c.* 1951. Left to right: William Standlake (patrolman), William Pratt (lengthman), Frank Marchant (sub-ganger), F.C. Hamnett (district engineer), Fred Tregay (lengthman), Frank Pinney (ganger), Sam Parkhouse (lengthman), Ron Smith (lengthman), Percy Pullen (inspector).

Guide Dogs for the Blind tableau, Exmouth Carnival, *c.* 1954.

Maria Gibbons, 1890. Maria Gibbons lived in Budleigh Salterton and was one of the town's most colourful characters. She travelled Devon in a horse and trap and wrote books on her adventures. She is pictured here leaving on one of her trips.

Royal Marines at a passing-out parade, Lympstone camp, 1958. No book on Exmouth would be complete without a picture of the Royal Marines.

Exmouth Boys Brigade outside Tower Street church, Exmouth, *c.* 1955. The Boys Brigade was founded in Glasgow in 1884. The Wesleyan Tower Street church was built in 1895.

'The Fire Service', Budleigh Salterton Carnival, 1956. Left to right: Charlie Jewell, Albert Hitt, Stan Alford, Bill Searle, Sid Malery, Jack Cooper.

The 5th St Andrew's Sea Scouts outside St Andrew's church, Exmouth, *c.* 1958. This may be an Empire Day celebration.

Street party, George V coronation celebrations, Budleigh Salterton, 1911. Those present include Albert Searle, Russell Baker, Doris Hutchings, Winnie Wish, Willie Baker and Harvey Mears.

Exmouth United AFC enjoyed a successful season in 1926/7 and are pictured here with their trophies. That year they were winners of the Peek Senior Shield, the Passmore Junior Shield and the Orchard cup.

Knocking down a pile of pennies collected for charity in the old Working Man's Club, Market Street, Exmouth. Mr Hocking and Mr Lynham are pictured here with other members.

SECTION SIX

Transport

Passengers waiting for a train to arrive, 1925. Like most seaside towns, Budleigh Salterton owes much of its development to the railway. The branch line from Exmouth that ran through Budleigh Salterton on its way to Sidmouth Junction lasted for sixty-four years.

The building of the railway line to Budleigh Salterton from a junction at Tipton St John was commemorated with a ceremony of cutting the first sod. The line opened on 15 May 1897. Celebrities attending included Mr Rempson, Sgt. Granger, Sir John Aird, Sir John Kennaway, Mrs Dora Merriam, Lady Rolle, Revd W.F. Green, Dr Walker, Lady Charmier Drummond, Sir Hugh Drummond, C.T.R. Roberts and Dr Brushfield.

Train for Exmouth arriving at Lympstone station, summer 1962.

The 2C55, the last train to leave Exmouth for Tipton St John, March 1967. The Budleigh Salterton railway opened in 1897 with the building of the line from Tipton St John. The line was extended to Exmouth and opened on 1 June 1903.

Crowds cheer the first train to Salterton station, 15 May 1897. The Budleigh Salterton railway began with the building of a line from a junction with the Sidmouth railway at Tipton St John.

Road repair gang, Knowle, *c.* 1906.

Mrs 'Donkey' Cowd, Budleigh Salterton, *c.* 1890.

Mrs 'Donkey' Cowd. Mrs Cowd kept her donkey in a field next to the school. She was what is often described as 'a character'.

Children from Budleigh Salterton on an excursion to Woodbury Common, *c.* 1902. The children were going on a picnic, and the little girls, with their splendid hats, were obviously wearing their best dresses.

Carriages at Woodbury Common, *c.* 1900. The meet on Woodbury Common always attracted a large number of spectators and included some of the first families in the county.

Steamroller belonging to the Exmouth Local Board, *c.* 1889.

Frank Watts, general carrier, Budleigh Salterton, *c.* 1910. Frank lived in Station Road with his daughters. Here he is with a fine-looking Foden steam lorry and one of his drivers, Mr T. Yeoman. Steam wagons were slow, cumbersome and heavy on coke, and were soon replaced by vehicles powered by the more efficient internal combustion engine.

One of the first service buses of the Devon General Bus Service, complete with driver and conductor. The company began operating in Exmouth after the First World War. The advertisement on the front of the bus is for Waltons, drapers, which had shops in Exeter and Exmouth. This bus was on the Exeter–Exmouth–Budleigh Salterton route.

Jigsaw dating from 1935. Such jigsaws were commonly sold in Exmouth at the time.

Queen Victoria's Diamond Jubilee celebration, outside the Coffee Tavern, Fore Street, Budleigh Salterton, 1897. The possibilities of a great celebration in 1897 were first discussed after the Jubilee of 1887, although it was not until 1896 that public interest in the great event was thoroughly aroused. Tuesday 22 June 1897 was observed as a Bank Holiday throughout the United Kingdom, and by that day nearly every street in the country was hung with decorations.

Bill Britton, driving a party of local people on a charabanc outing, 19 September 1922. His employer, Harris's Garage was in The Parade, Exmouth.

SECTION SEVEN

Sports

Players in an Exmouth Cricket Club charity match for the hospital, outside the pavilion, 1928. Front row, left to right: ? Puddicombe, ? Poole, ? Pengelly, ? Butt, -?-, ? Sidenham. Middle row: ? Emery, ? Skelton, ? Gibbins, ? Southwell, ? Willots, -?-, ? Kelland, -?-. Back row: -?-, ? Monk, -?-, ? Chown, ? Sercombe, -?-, ? Perry, ? Teal, ? Jeffreys.

Exmouth secondary modern school football team, 1960–1 season.

Phear Park Cricket Club, Exmouth, 1925. Cricket still retained its snobbishness in the 1920s, and this was a part of its appeal. Exmouth, like all towns, had its Gentlemen v. Players match, about which nobody felt uncomfortable.

Exmouth Swimming and Lifesaving Society members, 1931. The society initiated the 'Long Swim', the annual long distance swim from Exmouth to Starcross.

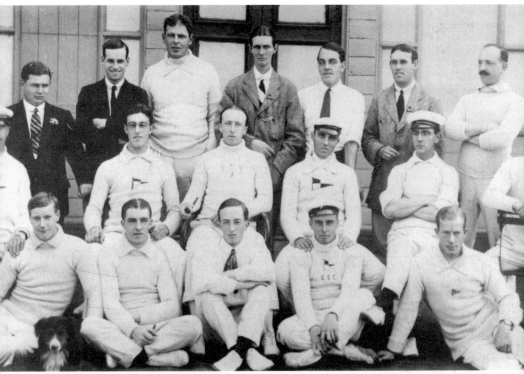

Checkstone Sailing Club, Exmouth, 1912. Outside the old pier pavilion are the founder members of the Checkstone Sailing Club, which is now known as the Exe Sailing Club. Front row, left to right: Doyle Stowell, Will Abbott, G.P. Perry, Reg Ward, Mr Gibbs. Middle row: Norman Mascall, Roy Dart, Reg Blackmore, Percy Matthews, Mr Cooper, George Beavis. Back row: Mr Godfrey, Bert Hooper, George Vinnicombe, Reg Abel, Mr Hooper, Gower Bennett.

Group of riders with their ponies, Woodbury Common.

Meet of the East Devon foxhounds, The Strand, Lympstone, *c.* 1960. The East Devon pack came into existence on 1 May 1890. Here the hunt is passing the old London Inn on the right. The butchers, W.H. White, in the foreground on the right is now a private house. At this time the kennels were at Clyst St Mary.

Lympstone Regatta and Sports, 1948. These are the participants in the 100 yard race, which was held in the Cliff Field.

The beach, Budleigh Salterton, c. 1959. Yachting, or, to use a more humble term, sailing, is a magnificent sport.

Budleigh Salterton football team celebrating a cup win, 1930s.

Sailors on Budleigh Salterton beach with their Heron class boat. Local waters and conditions provide a variety of problems for the yachtsman, and sailing, by its nature, attracts a special breed of person – an individualist with a great love of the sea.

The secondary modern school for boys, Exmouth, 1st XI 1956–7. Front row, left to right: R. Miller, A. Vincent, K. Parsons (capt.), G. Sydenham, T. Crees. Back row: D. Woodes, B. Tucker, J. Cowburn, H. Abbotts, I. Wilson, N. Bradford, J. Lyons.

Acknowledgements

I am grateful to the many people who have contributed material for this book. Particular thanks must go to the Fairlynch Museum, and especially Miss Joy Gawne, for supplying me with photographs and information about Budleigh Salterton. Members of Exmouth Museum and curator Bob Britton were most helpful, and I am indebted to them for the loan of material and a great deal of support. Special thanks must go to Miss Ursula Perry, who kindly helped by allowing me to use family photographs and giving me useful information. I am also grateful to Lyn Marshall for her help in the compilation of this collection, and to Roy Chapple, who gave much time in helping me with my enquiries. The accuracy of the facts in this book has been checked as carefully as possible. However, original sources can contain errors, and memories fade over the years. I would also like to add that the dates presented are mainly my own estimates, and may in some cases be over ten years out.

Finally, may I say that to live in old photographs is never to die.

E.S. Gosling

In the years following the 1914–18 war a major change was the coming of bus services and charabanc outings to all parts of the South West. Pictured here in 1924 are members of Exmouth Methodist church leaving the Parade in Exmouth for a trip to Cheddar.